W9-CAW-039

TERRORISM:
THE TARGET IS YOU!

The War Against
Radical Islam

By

Brigadier General Nick Halley
(U.S. Army, Retired)

Copyright ©2004 by Brigadier General
Nick Halley (U.S. Army, Retired)
First Edition

All rights reserved. Printed and bound in the U.S. No part of this book may be reproduced or transmitted in any form or by any means, electronic or mechanical, including photocopying, recording, or by an information storage and retrieval system—except by a reviewed who may quote brief passages in a review to be printed in a magazine or newspaper—without the written permission of the author. For information, please contact Brigadier General Nick Halley (U.S. Army, Retired) at 847-719-2637.

Although the author has made every effort to ensure the accuracy and completeness of the information contained in this book, I assume no responsibility for errors, inaccuracies, omissions, or any inconsistency herein. Any slights of people, places, or organizations are unintentional.

ISBN: 1-59196-759-7

Attention–Professional Organizations, Corporations and Colleges: Quantity discounts are available on bulk purchases of this book. For more information please contact Nick Halley at 847-719-2637

ACKNOWLEDGMENTS

My deepest thanks to the
following people and organizations:

The United States Military Academy at West Point, NY, where I learned honor and integrity, and where I developed as a man and soldier

The United States Army and all the great soldiers I've had the honor of serving with over many years of military service.

My son Matthew, who is my inspiration and my hero.

A very special personal thanks to Renee Conrad who encouraged me to start my writing and speaking career and provided me with continuous inspiration and encouragement.

Bob Kelly, my editor, who took a personal interest in the book and made many very helpful suggestions to improve it.

The many people in the National Speakers Association (NSA) – Illinois Chapter who provided help and encouragement every step of the way. Special thanks to Kevin O'Connor, the current President of the NSA-IL, who has been a mentor and friend.

DEDICATION

To my late father, Fred E. Halley,
who always supported me and encouraged me
to do my best. He was a great father who set the
example for me in every important area of life.
He was the best person I have ever known.

CONTENTS

Brigadier General Nick Halley

**General Halley and Bodyguards
Desert Storm**

General Halley and Saudi Prince

PREFACE

"Carelessness about our security is dangerous;
carelessness about our freedom is also dangerous."
Adlai E. Stevenson

We live in a very dangerous and confusing world. An international network of radical Muslim forces is threatening the world order by using terrorism as a strategy. It's very difficult for the average citizen to understand what's happening, because of incomplete and inaccurate news reporting by much of the media, and the distortion of information in our radicalized political system.

The purpose of this book is to explain in strong, simple, and sometimes politically incorrect ways, the background, strategy, significance, and potentially devastating effects of the essentially religious war we're fighting. The survival of our country and the free world depends on the forces of freedom winning this conflict.

I do *not* represent any political, social, or government organization. I'm not trying to convince the reader to adapt any particular political point of view. My purpose is to provide the reader with the perspective of a senior professional military officer who has had extensive experience leading thousands of our great soldiers in combat in Vietnam, Grenada, and Iraq, and has been a member of our anti-terrorist organizations.

Hopefully, the readers of this book will consider this perspective, along with other sources of information and their own religious, moral and political beliefs, to determine their individual views and convictions about this critically important conflict.

Chapters 1 and 2 address the background, uniqueness, dangers, and strategy for what I call World War IV — the war against radical Islam and the countries that support it. Chapter 3 provides an overview of the terrorists' organizations, objectives, goals, and probable future plans. Chapter 4 provides an assessment of the current status of the war and Chapter 5 discusses what we as citizens must do to make sure we win the war. Chapter 6 outlines the reasons why victory against terrorism is essential, and Chapter 7 emphasizes the need for strong leadership at every level in our nation.

My assessments are sometimes thought-provoking and controversial. There's a famous Chinese proverb that says: "May you live in interesting times." We live today in what are certainly among the most interesting and critical times in our country's history.

CHAPTER 1

WORLD WAR IV

"Once we have a war there is only one thing to do. It must be won. For defeat brings worse things than any that can ever happen in war."
Ernest Hemingway

"Let every nation know, whether it wishes us well or ill, that we will pay any price, bear any burden, meet any hardship, support any friend, oppose any foe, to assure the survival and success of liberty."
John F. Kennedy

"If we fail to realize that we're at war and don't take the appropriate actions now, it will be to our great peril, individually and as a nation."
Nick Halley

The United States of America and many other countries in the free world have joined forces to fight what I refer to as World War IV – the war against a global network of extreme Muslim radical forces and the countries that support these forces. The Cold War, which we won, was World War III.

World War IV is essentially a religious war against the radical Muslim extremists. It's not a war against the 1.5 billion Muslims in the world, or the Muslim religion. In fact, the great Muslim religion is being "hijacked" by these Muslim extremists. This war really started in 1979 when radical Iranian students captured the U.S. Embassy in Tehran, Iran. Most people failed to recognize that we were at war until the terrible attacks against the World Trade Center and the Pentagon in September 2001.

9/11 Attacks
The attacks against the World Trade Center in New York City and the Pentagon in Washington D.C. on September 11, 2001 profoundly changed our country and the world. For the first time in our nation's history, the vast expanses of the Atlantic and Pacific oceans were not enough to protect us from foreign attacks. The terrorists brought the fight to our soil on 9/11 and killed 3,000 innocent people in one day – including 235 non-U.S. citizens from 41 countries.

Our view of the world, our relationship with the United Nations, our economic policies, intelligence processes, judicial system and strategy were significantly affected – probably for the long term. The realization that we were subject to continued attacks in our own cities made most Americans more receptive to the concept of an aggressive foreign policy and to reassess and, at least temporarily, abridge some of our freedoms here at home in order to prevent future terrorist attacks in the U.S.

> *"Now and in the future, Americans will live*
> *as free people, not in fear, and never*
> *at the mercy of any foreign plot or power."*
> *President George W. Bush*

Paper Tiger? Or Sleeping Giant?
Why did the Al Qaeda leaders feel they could successfully attack us on 9/11? I see some parallels with the unprovoked surprise attack by Japanese aircraft on Pearl Harbor on December 7, 1941. That murderous attack, on what President Franklin D. Roosevelt called "a date which will live in infamy," claimed the lives of approximately 2,400 Americans.

At that time, Japanese leaders felt we were very vulnerable and a "paper tiger." After World War I, we had greatly reduced and disarmed our military. Soldiers conducted drills with wooden rifles because of a severe shortage of real weapons and ammunition.

The Japanese didn't think we had the will or capability to counter their surprise attack on Pearl Harbor. They hoped we wouldn't strongly react militarily, and would appease the expansion of the Japanese in East Asia or negotiate some deal favorable to them. However, as Admiral Isoroku Yamamoto,

Commander in Chief of the Imperial Japanese Navy and chief architect of the sneak attack, had predicted, they found out that, rather than being a "paper tiger," we were a "sleeping giant."

During the 1930s, Yamamoto had spent time in the U.S. Well aware of the capabilities of Americans, once they've been aroused, he was less eager for war than other senior Japanese leaders. As history would show, his fears were well grounded. Then once again, in September 2001, we were shamefully attacked, and our response must be no less powerful and conclusive than it was in World War II.

Sending the Wrong Signals

In the years prior to the 9/11 attacks, we gave our enemies many signals that we were again a "paper tiger," and could be attacked without strongly reacting. In November 1979, radical Shia students in Tehran, Iran overran our embassy and took 52 of our citizens hostage, holding them in captivity for 444 days. The response by the Carter administration was weak and indecisive.

Throughout the 1980s, with one exception, we failed to strongly react to numerous other terrorist attacks. On one occasion in 1986, President Reagan did direct an air strike against Colonel Muammar Kaddafi in Tripoli and Benghazi, Libya. That attack was very effective and did result in some future constraint on the part of Colonel Kaddafi.

In 1983, the U.S. Marine Barracks in Beirut, Lebanon was attacked with a car bomb, killing 257 marines. The U.S. response to that attack was to leave

Lebanon. The Syrians then filled the resulting political and military void, taking control of Lebanon and turning it into a hotbed of terrorist activities that continue to this day.

During this period, we considered terrorist attacks as criminal activities and issued ineffective "strongly worded diplomatic statements, resolutions, and indictments," which were harmless to the terrorists and encouraged them to increase the number and scope of their activities. From the terrorists' viewpoint, we were in fact "paper tigers."

Desert Storm

In 1991, Saddam Hussein, the President of Iraq, ordered the Iraqi Army to invade Kuwait. The U.S. led a coalition of countries, including many Muslim nations, to enforce a UN resolution to liberate Kuwait from Iraqi occupation. The resolution did not call for a march on Baghdad, the capital of Iraq, or an overthrow of Saddam. Our Arab and Muslim partners made it clear that the only purpose of this operation from their perspective and the UN perspective was to free Kuwait.

The U.S. and coalition forces conducted a very effective campaign – Desert Storm – against Saddam Hussein and liberated Kuwait in a 100-hour war. I was one of the general officer combat commanders during that war. Due to the limitations of the UN resolution and the somewhat fragile U.S./Arab/Muslim coalition, our American forces were not in a position to directly overthrow Saddam.

It was our hope that the operation would cause the overthrow of the Saddam Hussein government by an uprising among the liberated Iraqi Shia and Iraqi Kurds who had long been persecuted by the Sunni Muslim minority who supported Saddam.

Another U.S. goal was to weaken the Iraqi Army to the point that they would be no threat to their neighboring countries. However, we wanted to leave the Iraqi Army enough forces to protect their borders in the event Iran tried to take advantage of any Iraqi weakness. We were spectacularly successful in enforcing the UN resolution to free Kuwait, but we failed to accomplish our goal of overthrowing Saddam by a Shia/Kurd uprising.

Had our military been allowed to finish the job in Desert Storm by simply disarming the Republican Guard, it's clear to me that we would probably not be back in Iraq today.

Unfinished Business

Basically, at the end of the shooting war, we allowed the Iraqis to keep too many armed combat forces. To the surprise and shock of the American combat commanders at the time, we allowed the Republican Guard to return to the Baghdad area with their weapons. The Republican Guard immediately protected Saddam and killed thousands of the Shia and Kurds who were being encouraged by the U.S. to take control of Iraq and displace Saddam. In military terms, we "snatched defeat from the jaws of victory."

We suddenly departed Iraq within a week after the end of the shooting war and left the Shia and

Kurd forces that had cooperated with us and supported our efforts to a cruel fate. Had our military been allowed to finish the job in Desert Storm by simply disarming the Republican Guard, it's clear to me that we would probably not be back in Iraq today. It's no wonder many of the Kurd and Shia people in Iraq are not convinced we'll continue to support them in the current Iraqi conflict.

Our lack of response prior to the 9/11 attacks encouraged the terrorists to become bolder and to continue the frequency and intensity of their attacks.

In 1993, several events happened that reinforced the terrorist view that we were an "easy target" or "paper tiger," despite having the most powerful military in the world. The World Trade Center was bombed by Al Qaeda, killing six people and wounding several hundred others. Our response was again ineffective and weak.

"The peace of the man who has forsworn the use of the bullet seems to me not quite peace, but a canting impotence."
Ralph Waldo Emerson

Also in 1993, Saddam Hussein attempted to assassinate former President George H.W. Bush in Kuwait. President Clinton responded by firing a few

Cruise missiles at some unoccupied government building in Baghdad. Only a few night watchmen and cleaning people were impressed. The Arab press and the terrorists ridiculed the meager effort as a sign of weakness.

Disaster in Somalia

The most significant event from a terrorist viewpoint occurred in 1993 in Somalia. We went to that country with the purest of intentions – to restore order, end the civil war, and prevent the starvation of tens of thousands of Muslim people. The Muslim warlords were preventing international aid from being properly distributed to the starving people.

In an Army Ranger operation against one of these warlords, Mohammed Farah Aideed, a Blackhawk helicopter was shot down and 18 Americans were killed in the operation. This attack was chronicled in the movie *Blackhawk Down*. Our response was to leave Somalia.

This was the final event that persuaded the international terrorist leaders and their organizations – especially Osama Bin Laden and Al Qaeda – that the U.S. would not strongly respond militarily to terrorist attacks. Our lack of response prior to the 9/11 attacks encouraged the terrorists to become bolder and to continue the frequency and intensity of their attacks.

The terrorists became convinced that the most powerful country in the world had a very weak will. They were persuaded that we could be defeated in any conflict by turning American public opinion against a particular conflict simply by killing enough Americans over a period of time. In effect, the real target of the terrorist attacks is the American people. They want to break the will of the American people. *This so-called "Somalia Strategy" is the basis of their current strategy.*

The Most Difficult War

Many people don't seem to think we're at war. They feel the dozens of terrorist attacks since 1979 are criminal acts that should be treated as crimes and thus prosecuted in our courts. But make no mistake about it: *the radical Muslim groups (terrorists) are very definitely at war with us.* If we fail to realize we're at war, and don't take the appropriate actions now, it will be to our great peril, individually and as a nation.

"War is an ugly thing but not the ugliest of things; the decayed and degraded state of moral and patriotic feelings which thinks that nothing is worth war is much worse. A man who has nothing for which he is willing to fight, nothing which is more important than his own personal safety, is a miserable creature and has no chance of being free unless made and kept so by the exertions of better men than himself."
John Stuart Mill

The immediate threat to our country is the procurement and use of weapons of mass destruction (WMDs) – chemical, biological or nuclear weapons – by the terrorists, targeted against our major population centers. The United Nations has issued numerous reports that several international terrorist groups are aggressively trying to obtain WMDs.

Osama Bin Laden, the head of the terrorist group Al Qaeda, has stated publicly that the terrorists have "a holy obligation" to procure and use WMDs against the United States. If they're successful, the 3,000 people killed in one day on 9/11 at the World Trade Center and the Pentagon will be considered a relatively minor attack, when compared to the potentially hundred of thousands who would probably be casualties in a WMD attack.

> **We have never before faced an enemy that wanted simply to kill our citizens and are willing or even anxious to die in the process.**

Difficult, Dangerous – and Deadly!

In many ways, this is the most dangerous and difficult war in our history, for several reasons:

1. It's very hard to identify our enemies. They're embedded in the populations of more than 60 countries, including the United States. In many countries, they're protected by a significant portion of the population.

2. They want to kill us, and our children. On many occasions, Al Qaeda has published documents or played audio and video tapes in which they blame most of the problems of the Arab and Muslim world on the United States. In one of these documents by the Number

Two man in Al Qaeda, Ayman Al-Zawahari, they announced their goal to kill four million Americans, to include two million children. We have never before faced enemies who wanted simply to kill our citizens, even our children, and are willing or even anxious to die in the process.

3. We are no longer protected by the vast expanses of the Pacific and Atlantic oceans. Some of the battles in this worldwide war are being waged right here in the U.S. Not since the American Civil War has a conflict taken place on our soil.

4. This war will last a long time. There will probably not be a decisive battle, such as Gettysburg in the Civil War or the Normandy invasion in World War II, that will turn the tide of the war in the favor of the winner. This will test the will of the American people to the maximum. The normal impatience of our people to "win" and to find "immediate solutions" will result in severe frustration. We must be prepared for this war to last as long as 20 years or more. Our grandchildren will likely have to continue to fight it.

We *can* win this war, but it will take an all-out effort of the free world over a long period of time. Our strategy must be clear and forceful, and executed throughout the world with great skill and overwhelming force as required.

CHAPTER 2

A CONFLICT OF STRATEGIES

*"Thus, what is of supreme importance in war
is to attack the enemy's strategy."*
Sun-tzu

"The American people and their elected leaders
will continue to be faced with hard choices and difficult
moments, for resolve is continually being tested by those
who envy us our prosperity and begrudge us our freedom.
America will remain great and act responsibly so long as
it exercises power – wisely, and not in the bullying sense
– but exercises it, nonetheless."
Ronald Reagan

"The major conflict in the world today
is the clash of these two opposing strategies.
We are the only force that can stop
the Muslim extremists and they are
the only force that can stop us."
Nick Halley

To understand what's happening in the world today, the War against Radical Islam (War against Terrorism), it's essential that the high-level strategy for both sides is understood.

The terrorists' (Radical Islamic groups) over-riding main strategy is to convert the Muslim countries of the world to fundamentalist (Taliban-type) Muslim governments. Fundamentalist Muslim governments have no need for a Constitution. The Koran – Islam's holy book – is the focal point of all Muslims.

There are no elected politicians. The religious leaders are the leaders of the country. There's no separation of state and religion. The state is the religion and vice versa. Women live under very strict and inflexible Islamic laws that greatly abridge many of their basic human rights, such as voting and education.

The United States of America and our free-world allies want to change the governments of the world to democratic or representative-type governments. *The major conflict in the world today is the clash of these two opposing strategies. We are the only force that can stop the Muslim extremists and they are the only force that can stop us.*

The conflicts in Iraq, Afghanistan, Libya, Israel, Saudi Arabia, Lebanon, the U.S. and many other countries are battlegrounds or campaigns in the greater war. The "War in Iraq" is in reality not a separate war but the most visible of the current campaigns as part of the larger conflict.

"Hostility toward America is a religious duty,
and we hope to be rewarded for it by God ...
I am confident that Muslims will be able to end the
legend of the so-called superpower that is America."
Osama Bin Laden

Radical Muslim Strategy

To support their overall strategy, the radicals are using a tactic commonly employed when a weak military force encounters a much stronger one – terrorism. Since the radical Muslim forces cannot defeat the U.S. military in a more conventional war, they use their limited resources and combat power to conduct terrorist attacks. Terrorism tactics are characterized by hit-and-run attacks, car bombs, suicide attacks, roadside bombs, and kidnappings, in order to inflict the maximum damage against their enemies.

> **The terrorists' goal is to kill as many Americans and other 'non-believers' as possible in the hope and belief that the American people will lose the will to fight and withdraw from all Muslim countries.**

This ancient tactic has been used throughout the history of warfare in dozens of situations in many countries. The terrorists' goal is to kill as many Americans and other "non-believers" as possible, in the hope and belief that the American people will lose the will to fight and withdraw from all Muslim countries – the "Somalia Strategy" discussed in Chapter 1.

"Let us recollect that peace or war will not always be left to our option; that however moderate or unambitious we may be, we cannot count upon the moderation, or hope to extinguish the ambition of others."
Alexander Hamilton

If the Americans did withdraw from the Muslim countries, the terrorists would then be free to convert all those countries, one-by-one, to fundamentalist Muslim governments. This would effectively "enslave" a large percentage of the world population and prevent the advancement and education of millions of women.

The radical Muslims are determined to win. They are fully prepared – even anxious – to die for their cause.

Imagine a world where Al Qaeda-run countries control 75 percent of the world's oil reserves, have nuclear weapons, and tens of thousands of young men and women willing and anxious to die for their cause. The annihilation of Israel, probably with nuclear and chemical weapons, would be virtually assured.

The current conflicts in the Mideast are completely consistent with their strategy. In Iraq, they want to prevent the interim Iraq leaders from establishing a successful representative government. In

Saudi Arabia, they want to overthrow the Saudi Kingdom and establish a fundamentalist government. In Israel, they want to destroy the country and reestablish a fundamentalist Palestinian government. In short, they're using terrorist tactics and the "Somalia Strategy" to drive us out of the Muslim countries, so they can establish a fundamentalist Muslim government in all of them.

The radical Muslims are determined to win. They are fully prepared – even anxious – to die for their cause. They will not be deterred by appeasement, negotiations, or other "humane and civilized" acts on our part. *Our only realistic option is to adopt an offensive strategy that attacks the terrorists before they can attack us.*

"We make war that we may live in peace."
Aristotle

U.S. Strategy
Since the start of the "Cold War" with the Soviet Union in the 1960s, the U.S. has employed a strategy of deterrence in some form or other. This strategy called for the U.S. to stay strong, militarily, politically, and economically, so that any potential enemies would be afraid to attack our country. If they did attack, we would have the military strength to punish the attacker or win any resulting war. Although there were numerous regional wars throughout the world during this period, our national security was never really seriously threatened.

We won World War III – the Cold War – with

this deterrence strategy. The 96-mile-long Berlin Wall, which divided communist East Germany from democratic West Germany, was erected in 1961. This structure symbolized and was a part of the "Iron Curtain" which separated the communist Soviet Union from the rest of the world.

In November 1989, more than 28 years after the construction was completed, the Berlin Wall fell. Shortly thereafter, the second most powerful superpower in the world, the Soviet Union and its satellite countries, broke apart. One-by-one, the satellite countries declared their independence from Russia and formed their own governments.

The U.S. continued with the deterrence strategy from the end of the Cold War in 1989 until the year that profoundly changed our country: 2001. After the 9/11 attacks, we realized the strategy of deterrence was very ineffective against the terror-

The half-measures against terrorism tried in the 1980s and 1990s failed, and led to the devastating 9/11 attacks.

ists. The terrorists wanted to kill us and our children, and were willing and even anxious to die in that process. Deterrence simply does not work under those conditions.

"We love peace, but not peace at any price.
There is a peace more destructive of the manhood
of living man than war is destructive of his body.
Chains are worse than bayonets."
Douglas Jerrold

In addition, a policy of deterrence allows the enemy to strike first. Now that we were being attacked on our own soil, we could not continue with a strategy that allowed a first strike by our enemies. If the terrorists employed weapons of mass destruction (chemical, biological or nuclear) against our population centers, the resulting casualties would be catastrophic. Therefore, the era of a deterrence strategy in America has ended.

From years of terrorist attacks, one lesson is very clear. Appeasement, negotiations, conciliation and human kindness are seen as weakness by the terrorists and in fact encourage them to conduct even more attacks. With an enemy that wants to kill you and your family, there are only two choices: fight or appeasement. The half-measures against terrorism tried in the 1980s and 1990s failed and led to the devastating 9/11 attacks. We clearly needed a new strategy that would be effective against the international terrorist movement.

"The best form of defense is attack."
Karl von Clausewitz

Preemptive Strategy

The U.S. has now adopted a new strategy – the preemptive strategy. This is a very dangerous and risky strategy. Good intelligence information is critical to make this strategy viable. This strategy calls for the U.S. to attack any country or group that presents a "clear and present" danger to our country. The threat does not have to be imminent.

This strategy basically calls for us to hunt down and destroy any enemies before they strike — not after. This strategy also calls for the countries of the world to renounce terrorism and not provide support to the terrorists. Countries that align themselves with terrorists are also subject to attack as part of the preemptive strategy.

The invasions by the U.S.-led military coalitions in Afghanistan and in Iraq were preemptive strikes and key, important and necessary operations in the War on Terrorism.

The primary danger with this strategy that worries those of us who have served as wartime military leaders is that it isn't difficult to make a mistake and conduct a major military operation against a threat that turns out to be less than a "clear and present" danger. However, given the threat of attacks against a U.S. target with weapons of mass destruction, we cannot afford to err on the side of caution.

"America has entered a great struggle that tests our strength, and even more our resolve. Our nation is patient and steadfast. We continue to pursue the terrorists in cities and camps and caves across the earth. We are joined by a great coalition of nations to rid the world of terror. And we will not allow any terrorist or tyrant to threaten civilization with weapons of mass murder."
President George W. Bush

The invasions by the U.S.-led military coalitions in Afghanistan and in Iraq were preemptive strikes and key, important and necessary operations in the War on Terrorism.

In Afghanistan, Al Qaeda (the organization that conducted the 9/11 attacks against the U.S.) had large military training camps that trained more than 20,000 terrorists. In addition, Afghanistan was being brutally ruled by a radical fundamentalist Muslim government, the Taliban, which protected Al Qaeda and provided them a sanctuary.

In my view, the fact that we have not had any major terrorist attacks in the U.S. since 9/11 has been primarily due to our new aggressive offensive strategy that has kept the terrorists off balance and on the defensive.

This invasion was necessary to break up the Al Qaeda training network and put its leadership on the run and on the defensive, and to replace the Taliban government with a legitimate representative government chosen by the Afghan people.

Iraq and 9/11

There is no strong evidence of a direct involvement by Iraq with the 9/11 attacks. However, the 9/11 Commission confirmed that Iraq had maintained a relationship with Al Qaeda and other terrorist organizations for many years. In fact, in 1998, the Clinton

Administration indicted the Al Qaeda leader, Osama Bin Laden, charging that he and Iraq had reached an understanding on a number of joint projects.

Russian President Vladimir Putin, who was opposed to the Iraqi invasion, stated in June 2004 that his intelligence agencies had received information that Iraq was planning multiple terrorist attacks against the U.S. in early 2002 – before the invasion.

Iraq was clearly a major part of the overall international terrorist network. To defeat this network and win the War on Terrorism, we must take action against the entire network – not just the specific organization that attacked us on 9/11. For example, the Mafia could not be eliminated by concentrating on only one Mafia family.

We believed Saddam would not hesitate to provide weapons of mass destruction, support, sanctuary, money and knowledge to the international terrorist organizations. It was important to defeat Saddam Hussein and his Baath Party government, so they could no longer provide any type of support to the international terrorist movement.

In addition, Saddam's defiance of 17 UN Security Council resolutions, his alleged (still under investigation) weapons of mass destruction programs, and his criminal mistreatment of the Iraqi people made him a legitimate target.

In my view, the fact that we have not had any major terrorist attacks in the U.S. since 9/11 has been primarily due to our new aggressive offensive strategy that has kept the terrorists off balance and on the defensive.

This preemptive strategy is being carried out at several different levels. In the short term, in cooperation with other countries, we must 'root out" the terrorists and attack them or arrest them throughout the world. This will be a difficult job because the terrorists are embedded in the populations of more than 60 countries – including the U.S. Our invasion of Afghanistan is the best large-scale example of directly attacking the terrorists in their sanctuaries.

> **Our long-term objective is to change the governments in the Muslim and Arab world to some type of democratic or representative government. We will not win World War IV until we are successful.**

However, this effort is being done on a smaller scale in many countries, including the U.S. Because we cannot possibly find and attack the entire embedded terrorist organizations – particularly the ones in countries that are harboring and supporting terrorists – we must use our full economic and political power to fight terrorism worldwide.

Cutting Off Support

In the midterm, we must take strong action to convince or prevent countries – particularly in the Mideast – from supporting terrorism. The terrorists vitally need support from rogue countries – a base – to provide sanctuaries, safe areas, training facilities and money. This support is critically important to the terrorists in order to be able to properly train, equip, plan, integrate new people into the organization, and conduct large-scale terrorist attacks worldwide.

One of the main purposes of going into Iraq was to establish a powerful American military presence in the Mideast in the geographical center of the countries that support terrorism. This intimidating U.S. presence in the middle of the Islamic world puts us in a strong position to convince, coerce or prevent those countries from continuing their support of terrorism. This would be much more difficult for us to accomplish from the U.S. – thousands of miles away.

Countries in the Mideast that support terrorism include (but are not limited to) Syria, Iran, Pakistan, Saudi Arabia and, until recently, Libya. A critical part of our strategy is to stop these countries from supporting terrorism. As a last resort, we might have to use military force in the future to accomplish this critical objective.

Working Toward Change

Our long-term objective is to change the governments in the Muslim and Arab world to some type of democratic or representative governments. We will not win World War IV until we are successful in converting the vast majority of these Mideast countries and in solving the Israel-Palestinian problem (a future book).

These governments do not have to be modeled on the U.S. or British systems. Each country can develop its own form of representative government by integrating its key tribal or regional customs, or ethnic realities, into its own design. The only real requirement from our perspective is that each government be elected by the people, and respect and protect the basic rights of the people. It's also critical that these governments join the free nations of the world in peace and harmony.

The forces of the free world have been converting countries to representative governments since early in the 20th century. In 1917, during the World War I era, there were only about 10-12 democracies in the entire world. Today about 120 of the 192 countries in the world have some form of representative government. We've made these conversions against seemingly impossible odds.

After World War II, few people would have believed that Japan, ruled by an emperor who was considered "divine," and with almost no democratic history, could possibly be converted to a democracy – but it was, with the help and guidance of General Douglas MacArthur and a massive U.S. rebuilding effort.

Also after World War II, West Germany and later East Germany each converted to a representative form of government, despite years under Hitler and the Nazi regime. More recently, we've witnessed the fall of the Soviet Union empire. Contrary to the expectations of many "experts," Russia and all but two of the satellite countries have converted to various forms of representative government.

The Task Ahead

We must now convert the Muslim and Arab world to

representative governments. Many people believe there's something about the Muslim religion that precludes Muslim countries from adopting a representative-type government. This is simply not correct.

Of the 1.5 billion Muslims in the world today, more than half of them already live in a country with some type of representative government. Bangladesh, Indonesia, Pakistan, India, the U.S., France, and Turkey (plus many others) all have large Muslim populations. The United States alone has 9.7 million Muslims.

The task of converting these Muslim countries is going to probably take 10-20 years. Currently there are 22 Arab countries, none of which has a representative government. Of the 24 Muslim but non-Arab countries, about half have representative governments. Israel and Turkey (and soon Iraq) are the only democracies in the Mideast. Most rulers in this region are various types of dictators. They either "rule from God" (Iran), or from genealogy (Saudi Arabia), or from the "barrel of a gun" (Syria, Libya, and until recently, Iraq).

Ripe for Change
The Mideast is ripe for political change. This region has five percent of the world population but represents only two percent of the world economy. Many of these countries have vast wealth in the form of oil but their people live at a substandard level due to ineffective and corrupt governments.

Unemployment is over 20 percent in many of these countries. Wealth is not distributed to the people but is centralized with the dictators, and their families and key followers.

The dictators in this region are not willing to die for their countries or "causes." They have three priorities: stay in power, stay in power, and stay in power. Their military and police forces aren't strong, because they choose their leaders for their political connections rather that their ability. These military forces are also ineffective against other armies, because they're trained to prevent change, control the population and prevent the overthrow of their dictators.

Perhaps the odds of converting these governments – especially the Arab governments – are not high. This will be a long and difficult undertaking but the potential gains are enormous: the end of terrorism, plus a more stable world and the release of millions of women from the restraints of the radical Muslim movement.

CHAPTER 3

INSIDE TERRORISM

"A republic will avoid war unless the avoidance might create conditions that are worse than warfare itself. Sometimes, the dispositions of those who choose to make themselves our enemies leave us no choice."
Thomas Jefferson

"The enemies who struck us
are determined and they are resourceful.
They will not be stopped by a sense of
decency or a hint of conscience –
but they will be stopped."
President George W. Bush

"From the mid-1990s forward,
a small group of deadly, radical terrorists
emerged. These terrorists want to kill
their victims. They do not want to negotiate.
They do not fear death.
In fact, many of them welcome death."
Nick Halley

The Muslim religion is separated into two major factions – the Sunni Muslims and the Shia Muslims. The split between the Sunnis and Shias has a long and complicated theological basis, dating back more than thirteen centuries to the role of Ali, following the death of Mohammed in 633 A.D. Ali, a cousin of Mohammed's, was recognized by the Shias as his successor. However, the Sunnis believed that Ali was fourth in line after Mohammed (rather than first in line), signaling the start of the hostility that continues to this day.

The radical elements of both the Sunnis and Shias are very harsh, determined, and deadly.

Approximately 85 percent of the 1.5 billion Muslims are Sunnis. Shias are located in every Muslim nation, but they are mainly concentrated in Iran, Iraq (60 percent of the Iraqi population), Yemen, and Azerbaijan.

Both the Sunnis and Shias believe in the Muslim Holy Book, the Koran. Both sides recognize the other faction as legitimate Muslims. However, there's a long history of the Sunnis and Shias fighting each other. In fact, the minority Sunni population in Iraq (15 percent of the total population) under Saddam Hussein dominated and persecuted the majority Shias for many years.

The Shias have powerful clergy who often provide strong religious and political guidance to their followers. The Sunnis have clergy but they're considered more as religious scholars and respected teachers. However, the radical elements of both the Sunnis and Shias are very harsh, determined, and deadly.

The terrorists are a worldwide network of radical Muslim groups, supported by several rogue countries. The radicals belong to three different major categories or groups. Each major group has a multitude of splinter and associated sub-groups. All three major groups are radical Muslims located in the Middle East.

The radical Shia of Iran are a major terrorist force that must be neutralized or destroyed before we can win the War on Terrorism.

They all hate the U.S. and Israel, and any country or group that supports the two countries. They also hate each other and have fought against each other in the past. However, they have put their hatred of each other on hold while they fight their common enemy – the United States.

"Men never do evil so completely...as when they do it from religious conviction."
Blaise Pascal

Major Muslim Radical Groups

There are three major Muslim radical groups operating today: the Radical Islamic Shias; the Baath Party Fascists; and the Radical Sunnis. While they share a hatred of the United States and its allies, each has conducted its own campaign of terror against their common enemy.

- **Radical Islamic Shias:** Iran is predominately a Shia nation with a fundamentalist government ruled by the Ayatollahs. There are elections in Iran but the major power is in the hands of the non-elected clergy. Basically, the reign of terror was started in 1979 by the radical Iranian students who overran the U.S. Embassy in Tehran, Iran and held our embassy personnel hostage for 444 days.

The Iranians have conducted or supported many terrorist attacks worldwide, including the bombing of the U.S. Marine Barracks in Lebanon in 1983. Many terrorist attacks against Israel were conducted by the group Hezbollah – an Iranian-backed group.

The Iranians are suspected of supporting some of the attacks against the U.S. in Iraq. They definitely are supporting the radical Iraq cleric Muqtada Al-Sadr, who led a series of unsuccessful Shia rebellions in southern Iraq. The radical Shia of Iran are a major terrorist force that must be eventually neutralized or destroyed before we can win the War on Terrorism.

> **Al Qaeda remains the most immediate threat to the U.S. homeland, and will probably be the most difficult force to defeat.**

There's a real chance that the radical government in Iran will eventually implode. Its economy is very weak and completely dependent on oil revenues. There's much unrest among the students and the intellectual elite. The radical religious people are still firmly in control but are being forced to make some concessions and political reforms. These conditions might eventually fuel a revolution against the radical Iranian Ayatollahs.

- **Baath Party Fascists:** Iraq (now neutralized) and Syria are countries ruled by fascist dictators. Both are Muslim countries, but religion takes a "back seat" to the iron-fisted rule of the dictators. Iraq was clearly a part of the international terrorist network before its fall. Syria remains one of the primary countries that support terrorism. Many Syrian fighters have joined the various radical Muslim groups throughout the Mideast.

  Syria, in effect, controls Lebanon, where numerous terrorist groups live and work with the permission and support of Syria. It's also likely that Syria harbors many illegal weapons (based on UN resolutions forbidding certain weapons), and possibly weapons of mass destruction from Iraq.

  We still have some power and leverage over Syria. The Israeli army is on one side of Syria, and a U.S. Army Division is just across its border with Iraq. We could also severely damage its economy with a UN economic boycott.

- **Radical Sunnis:** Al Qaeda and the Taliban are

prime examples of radical Sunni terrorist groups. Al Qaeda believes in the Wahabi view of Islam. This is a fundamentalist, ultra-conservative movement that started more than 200 years ago. This movement brought the believers back to the fundamentals of the Muslim teachings. They believe in very strict adherence to Muslim law.

Saudi Arabia is the center and financial base of Wahabi terrorism. Wahabism has always tolerated and even encouraged killing infidels or non-believers. Wahabis have little tolerance or flexibility in their strict religious views. They are completely willing to die for their cause.

Al Qaeda has been responsible for dozens of attacks against the U.S. or our allies. Some prime examples are: the World Trade Center bombing in February 1993 which resulted in six deaths; the October 2000 attack on the USS Cole in the Port of Yemen, killing 17; and the September 11, 2001 attacks against the World Trade Center and the Pentagon, where nearly 3,000 died.

Al Qaeda remains the most immediate threat to the U.S. homeland, and will probably be the most difficult force to defeat. It has extensive monetary support, primarily from Saudi Arabia, and has highly organized affiliated groups in at least 30 countries, including the United States.

Their Objectives and Goals
Until the mid-1990s, the terrorists generally had

some set of demands. They wanted to negotiate something. They were willing to kill their victims when necessary but they wanted attention, publicity, or TV time, in order to accomplish their specific goals. These goals were generally money, release of political prisoners, political concessions, or more political control. They did not want to die.

From the mid–1990s forward, a small group of deadly, radical terrorists emerged. These terrorists want to kill their victims. They do not want to negotiate. They do not fear death. In fact many of them welcome death. They conduct their attacks because they feel that God has commanded them to do so.

Their overall goals, as discussed in Chapter 2, are to drive the U.S. forces from Muslim soil and convert the Muslim countries to fundamentalist governments.

Why They Hate Us

The primary reason the terrorists hate us is because we are the only force with the power and will to stop their radical movement from converting countries to fundamentalist governments.

In 2002, the deputy leader of Al Qaeda, Al-Zawahiri, wrote in a well-publicized document titled, "In the Shadow of the Lances," that America is the reason for all oppression, injustice, licentiousness, or suppression that is the Muslims' lot. "It (America) stands behind all the disasters that were caused and are still being caused to the Muslims." Clearly we are blamed for all of the Muslims' problems.

They are totally outraged that we have a military presence in the Muslim world. They will not stop their attacks as long as one American soldier remains on Muslim soil.

They also hate us for our continued support of Israel. The U.S. Government has tried to be seen as a neutral party in negotiations between Israel and the Palestinians. However, from the Muslim perspective, the U.S. has sided with Israel on almost every important issue. The elimination of Israel is a driving force on the mind of every radical terrorist.

Finally, they are afraid our strong culture will be adopted by their population. Our culture tends to overwhelm and smother other cultures. They want to totally control their population and to have no outside influences. They especially fear freedom of speech, freedom of religion, and freedom and equal treatment of women.

> **The elimination of Israel is a driving force on the mind of every radical terrorist.**

Osama Bin Laden

Osama was born in 1957 in Saudi Arabia into a very wealthy Saudi family. He was the 17th of 52 children. He had a normal life as a young man and graduated from college with a civil engineering degree. Osama is a very imposing 6' 5" tall and weighs about 160 pounds. He has three wives and a number of children.

Osama left the comforts of his home and a lavish lifestyle to go to Afghanistan in 1980 to fight the Russian occupation. From 1980 to 1986, he fought bravely against the Russians and won the admiration of the radical Muslim community. He was very instrumental in providing millions of dollars of support to the Muslim rebels, primarily from rich Saudi businessmen.

After the Afghan war, he returned to Saudi Arabia where he became very outspoken against the Saudi royal family. In about 1988 he formed the group, Al Qaeda, with Muslim extremists he fought with in the Afghan war against Russia. These recruits were from many different Mideast countries.

The initial purpose of Al Qaeda was to overthrow the House of Saud – the Saudi royal family. Just before the first Gulf War – Desert Storm – Osama became outraged that the Saudi royal family was allowing the build-up of American forces in Saudi Arabia – the sacred home of Mecca and Medina. He became so outspoken that the Saudi government expelled him from the country to Sudan, where he stayed for five years.

Osama continued to recruit, build, and train the Al Qaeda organization in Sudan. He planned and conducted several terrorist attacks while in Sudan, including the attack on the World Trade Center in 1993, and numerous terrorist attacks in Africa and the Mideast. Finally, in 1996, Sudan expelled Osama because of the intense pressure put on the government to arrest or turn him over to the U.S. or other western powers.

Osama went back to Afghanistan with the aid

and support of the fundamentalist government that had taken over that country – the Taliban. Osama established several terrorist training camps in Afghanistan and proceeded to train more than 20,000 potential terrorists from 1996 to 2001. He was again well-funded by wealthy Saudi businessmen throughout this period. In 2000, he directed the attack against the USS Cole. His "shining moment" came on September 11, 2001, with the devastating attacks on the World Trade Center in New York City and the Pentagon in Washington, D.C.

Osama had become a hero in most of the Muslim world. From their viewpoint, he had given up a lavish lifestyle to champion radical Muslim causes. He has attacked the most powerful country in the world, yet he remains free for the moment. He is still actively directing and leading Al Qaeda in planning and executing terrorist attacks all over the world, including many attacks against U.S. forces in Iraq.

Al Qaeda
As previously stated, Al Qaeda is devoted to the establishment of fundamentalist governments throughout the Muslim world. Before the 9/11 attacks, Al Qaeda was a very centralized organization, with its base in Afghanistan. The invasion of Afghanistan in late 2001 severely disrupted its operations. The large training camps in Afghanistan were destroyed and at least half of the organization and its leadership were killed or captured. However, they were not destroyed.

It's probable that the remaining Al Qaeda

headquarters and the senior leaders – to include Osama Bin Laden – are operating in the vast, mountainous, tribal-controlled, no-man's-land near the Afghanistan-Pakistan border. They have training camps in Somalia and Pakistan, and allied terrorist groups in 30-50 countries.

As a result of the successful Afghanistan campaign, Al Qaeda has reinvented itself, and is now much more decentralized. It's now an "umbrella" organization with a centralized planning cell and decentralized operations. The centralized cell, directed by Bin Laden, provides strategic planning, inspiration, and funding.

Al Qaeda has been badly weakened, but is still very dangerous and represents the most likely terrorist threat to the U.S. homeland.

Al Qaeda is now more a "movement" or an "ideology" than a highly structured organization. The relatively independent Al Qaeda affiliated or "franchised" terrorist groups or cells, located in 30-50 countries (including the U.S.), conduct their attacks based partially on the centralized guidance from Al Qaeda and partially based on their own determination of what terrorist attacks are appropriate in their countries.

Al Qaeda has been badly weakened, but is still very dangerous and represents the most likely terrorist threat to the U.S. homeland. Based on the coverage in the Arab press and statements from the Al Qaeda leaders, the terrorists still see us as weak and vulnerable, despite the successful invasions of Afghanistan and Iraq. They remained convinced that they can break the will of the American people by killing as many Americans – military and civilian – as possible over time.

Our difficulties in suppressing the insurgency in Iraq, and our recent negotiation strategy in Fallujah and with Al-Sadr (the radical Shia leader in Iraq who led an effective but unsuccessful rebellion against the U.S. in southern Iraq), are seen as terrorist victories by the Arab press and the terrorists. Appeasement, negotiations, western standards of restraint, and human kindness are uniformly seen as weakness in the Muslim world. Our military and political leaders must learn this lesson.

> **Appeasement, negotiations, western standards of restraint, and human kindness are uniformly seen as weakness in the Muslim world. Our military and political leaders must learn this lesson.**

"Our contest is not only whether we ourselves shall be free, but whether there shall be left to mankind an asylum on earth for civil and religious liberty."
Samuel Adams

Future Terrorist Plans
It is critical for Al Qaeda leaders and the other international terrorist organizations to effectively communicate with the Muslim population and with their

other allied terrorist groups and cells. They must keep the Muslim population informed of their progress and existence, so their recruiting efforts and support in the Muslim world will remain strong. They must communicate with their other terrorist groups to keep the morale high, transmit orders, and inform the groups about current and future terrorist strategies.

The telephone and other electronic means are seldom used by the terrorists, due to our ability to intercept their transmissions and pinpoint their locations. They use couriers, but they're subject to capture. Their favorite and most effective method of communications is sending video and audio tapes to the various Arab television stations, so the widest audience can hear and see the terrorist leaders directly.

Osama Bin Laden and his Al Qaeda deputy commander, Al-Zawahiri, have provided more than a dozen of these tapes to Arab TV within the past two years. The terrorists know we carefully study all these messages. In some cases, the messages target the American population as well as the Muslim population.

It's quite possible that the terrorists sometimes send lies or disinformation in these messages to confuse our intelligence efforts. However, in the past, these video and audio messages have very accurately predicted what the current and future strategies of the terrorists are.

Current Strategies

Based on their latest messages and their actions in various parts of the world, it's clear that the terrorists' current strategies to support their overall strategy of converting the Muslim countries to fundamentalist governments are:

To seek weapons of mass destruction (chemical, biological and nuclear) and use those weapons against major population centers. Osama Bin Laden has been quoted on several occasions that the terrorists have a "holy obligation" to procure and use these weapons. A UN report issued in December 2003 stated that the terrorist organizations are doing everything possible to acquire weapons of mass destruction. They have the money to procure these weapons and they definitely have the will to use them.

> **A UN report issued in December 2003 stated that the terrorist organizations are doing everything possible to acquire weapons of mass destruction.**

The use of these weapons against the countries that oppose terrorism is the most immediate threat to the U.S. and our allies. Based on other Al Qaeda messages, New York, Washington D.C., and Los Angeles are the primary targets.

To continue the terrorist resistance in Iraq and Afghanistan. Their plan is to terrorize the people so they will not participate in the political process, and disrupt our efforts to establish representative governments in those countries.

To direct terrorist attacks on the Muslim regimes in the Mideast that are cooperating with the U.S. operations in Iraq and Afghanistan. Saudi Arabia is the primary target, followed by Turkey, Pakistan, Bahrain, and Kuwait. They hope to seriously disrupt those governments and to eventually overthrow them.

To intimidate European nations so they will not cooperate with the U.S. in the Iraq or Afghanistan campaigns. The March 2004 terrorist attacks in Spain were very successful. These attacks clearly intimidated the Spanish electorate and were a major factor in the Spanish people voting out the previous regime that had supported the Iraq campaign by sending soldiers to Iraq.

The new prime minister has now withdrawn all Spanish troops from Iraq. This was a major win for the terrorists. The appeasement of the terrorists by the Spanish people will encourage the terrorists to redouble their efforts and conduct future attacks in Europe.

The Spanish pullout in Iraq reminds me of a situation just prior to World War II, when British Prime Minister Neville Chamberlain returned from a meeting with Adolf Hitler after signing the Munich Pact that basically appeased the German dictator's expansionist plans. Winston Churchill, then a Member of Parliament who was destined to replace Chamberlain as Prime Minister after the failure of the appeasement policy, told him: "You were given the choice between war and dishonor. You chose dishonor and now you will have war."

The Spanish people are in for more terrorist attacks because Osama Bin Laden sees them as weak, and because he has said that Spain was once Muslim and would be Muslim again some day.

In April 2004, Bin Laden, for the first time, offered a deal with the European countries that opposed his movement. Osama offered them a "truce," as long as they would withdraw all troops from Islamic countries and stop attacking Muslims. The Spanish people have opened up a "Pandora's Box" that will be difficult to close.

• **To kill Americans.** As mentioned previously, the terrorists have employed the "Somalia Strategy," which is to kill as many Americans as possible over time, in the hope that the American people will withdraw their support and the terrorists will win without the need to defeat our military. The terrorist leader Al-Zawahiri in, "In the Shadow of the Lances," declared that the radicals have the right to kill four million Americans, including two million children, in retaliation for his perception of our crimes in the Muslim world (Iraq, Afghanistan, Somalia, and other countries).

"Only the dead have seen the end of war."
Plato

What Lies Ahead
Based on a volume of information from Al Qaeda and other sources, Al Qaeda is definitely planning to

conduct additional terrorist attacks in the U.S. in the near- and mid-term. The terrorists hope to eventually attack U.S. targets with WMDs (chemical, biological, or nuclear). If they are successful these attacks would be devastating, causing tens of thousands of casualties. This is the most significant threat facing the U.S. in our recent history. Several terrorist plots have already been disrupted by U.S. counter-terrorist organizations. However, it's unlikely that we will continue to have a 100 percent success rate in preventing or disrupting planned attacks. Future successful terrorist attacks against U.S. targets are inevitable. We must be prepared for these attacks both physically and mentally.

Al Qaeda needs to conduct an attack in the U.S. in order to increase its credibility in the Muslim world. The terrorists are particularly interested in conducting attacks designed to influence U.S. elections. Their successful attacks in Spain, which resulted in the "hard-line" Spanish government losing the national elections to a government that is "soft" on terrorism, gave the terrorists hope and encouragement that this tactic could succeed in America.

Bringing down any high-level American official – especially a U.S. president – would greatly increase the prestige and political position of Al Qaeda throughout the entire world.

"The clever combatant imposes his will on the enemy, but does not allow the enemy's will to be imposed on him."
Sun-tzu, The Art of War

CHAPTER 4

ARE WE WINNING?

*"It is the object only of war that makes it honorable.
And if there was ever a just war since the world began,
it is this in which America is now engaged."*
Thomas Paine

"There is no security, no safety, in the appeasement of evil. It must be the core of Western policy that there be no sanctuary for terror. And to sustain such a policy, free men and free nations must unite and work together."
Ronald Reagan

"Those in this country who oppose the war need to realize they are unwittingly playing into the terrorists' hands. In some ways, their opposition is a greater danger to our losing the war than the actions of the terrorists."
Nick Halley

We *are* winning World War IV, the War on Terrorism, but there are many unresolved problems and many battles to fight before the final outcome is determined. Here are some of the major issues we're facing:

- We must stabilize Iraq and establish an Iraqi government accepted by the Iraqi people and recognized by the UN and by other Muslim countries.
- We must settle the Israeli–Palestinian problem (not discussed in this book).
- We must prevent the terrorists from destabilizing our allies in the Mideast and Europe – especially Israel, Saudi Arabia, and Pakistan.
- We must prevent Iran, North Korea, and Syria from supporting terrorism.

We are doing better in the global war against the radical Muslim groups than most citizens think. *Unfortunately, the bad news is being over-reported, while the good news is being under-reported.* This is causing great confusion and creating divisions in American public opinion that is significantly reducing public support for this critical war. This continuing erosion of support – not defeats on the battlefield – could cause us to eventually lose this war. The enemy is counting on this.

I totally agree that every American has the right and obligation to speak out on any issue. However, those in this country who oppose the war need to realize they are unwittingly playing into the terrorists' hands. In some ways, their opposition is a greater danger to our losing the war than the actions of the terrorists.

News Reporting

The "embedded reporters" did a great job of fairly reporting the news during the combat or "desert fighting" phase of the recent Iraqi war. Embedded reporters are regular reporters from print, TV and radio media who are assigned to a specific military organization for the duration of the conflict. They live with their assigned military units 24 hours a day.

As a result, the reporting of key stories during the war had a critical ingredient normally missing from wartime reporting – context. The reporters were able to put their current stories in context, because they were able to see the whole picture of what was happening in a military organization, and how that story related to the "big picture."

After the combat phase of the war ended and Baghdad fell, the embedded reporter program ended. *The quality, accuracy, objectivity, and fairness of the reporting on the War against Terrorism then took a giant turn for the worse.* Without embedded reporters, news people typically come to military units for a short time to focus on a specific story.

In many cases in Iraq, due to the poor security situation, the reporters seldom personally come to the military units to gather information. They get the daily Reuters and Associated Press accounts of the major events in Iraq and base their stories on the information in those releases. If any of us in the U.S. subscribed to those same news services, we could give the exact same reports right in our homes.

"The media are far more powerful than the President in creating public awareness and shaping public opinion, for the simple reason that the media always have the last word."
Richard M. Nixon

Many well-known reporters in Baghdad very seldom do any actual reporting by going into danger zones. When they give their reports based on information from the news services, they're careful to have a Baghdad scene in the background for their on-air reports, creating a false impression that they're reporting from the scene of the news.

Under these conditions, it's very difficult for reporters to see how their stories relate to the big picture, or how those stories fit into the overall situation. As a result, their stories are often one-sided, narrow, incomplete, and create false impressions.

Of course, there are exceptions. Some reporters routinely take great personal risks to get the story accurately. These reporters can be identified by their presence in the field among the soldiers at the location where a dangerous story is taking place.

One primary reason for the poor reporting is simply commercial competition. The hundreds of newspapers, magazines, and radio and TV stations are competing for ratings by presenting the more sensational stories in the most dramatic ways. Many of the reporters aren't interested in establishing a context for their stories – they just want to get their stories noticed by their managers in the U.S. so that their stories appear in the news. As I said earlier in this chapter, *this results in good news being grossly under-reported and bad news being grossly over-reported.*

Media Bias

Many media outlets have a definite political bias and deliberately slant the news based on that bias.

In addition, many media outlets have a definite political bias and deliberately slant the news based on that bias. I fully support our citizens expressing their political beliefs in forceful ways in the TV, radio or print media, as long as it's clear that they're expressing their opinions only.

"Iraq is getting taller and healthier every day, but those responsible for documenting the growth are not noticing — or if they are, they're not telling the people back home."
Noah D. Oppenheim

The big scandal is that many prominent well-known and respected network TV anchor people and newspaper and magazine writers present themselves as unbiased members of the "fourth estate," who are working on behalf of the American people to present the news in a fair and balanced way. *Unfortunately, a large number of them are clearly slanting and editing the news based on their own political beliefs.*

"The chief danger which threatens the influence and honor of the press is the tendency of its liberty to degenerate into license."
James A. Garfield

I believe citizens should use a wide variety of sources, including network news and the major newspapers, to gather information, so they can make informed decisions. However, many of these news organizations are very poor sources if you want unbiased, fair, and balanced information. Our citizens should certainly not rely on any single source of information.

It's human nature to listen to those sources that agree with our views, However, our citizens must gather information from a wide range of sources representing various opinions and insights, and then carefully weigh that information to arrive at well-informed conclusions, in order to accurately assess what's currently happening in this global War on Terrorism.

Partisan Politics

Our political parties have become radicalized. Leaders from both parties seem to hate one another and want to politically destroy one another. This has resulted in our political debates more closely resembling wars that legitimate political dialogue. Many politicians seeking office are distorting the news and emphasizing the bad news for their own purposes. Many trying to stay in office are "spinning" the news to their advantage.

As a result, it's difficult for the average citizen to determine the truth. As citizens, we should listen to the comments and opinions of our elected leaders on the issues; however, we must realize that we are oftentimes hearing partisan "spin."

Unfortunately, politicians are not always a reliable source of information. Again, it's critical that our citizens gather information from a wide variety of sources in order to be well informed. The Internet is one source that should not be overlooked.

There are many reasons to be cautiously optimistic – significant progress has been made.

Progress in the War
World War IV – the war against radical Islam (War on Terrorism) – is a struggle that will last many years, possible decades. The final history of the war will not be written for many years. Since we are in the early stages of this war, the progress is difficult to assess. However, there are many reasons to be cautiously optimistic – significant progress has been made. Following are a few key examples.

United States
We have not had a terrorist attack here in the U.S. for nearly three years (as of August 2004). This has been due primarily to our aggressive offensive strategy against terrorists worldwide. This offensive strategy has kept the terrorists off guard and made it more difficult for them to plan and execute operations in the

U.S.

In addition, our Department of Homeland Security, the Patriot Act, and law enforcement initiatives have added to our ability to prevent terrorist attacks. However, we are still an open country and are vulnerable to future attacks.

United Nations

The United Nations passed a resolution that calls on the member nations to support the reconstruction of Iraq and the formation of an elected Iraqi government. Although the level of support from many key UN member countries has been disappointing, we do have a resolution.

Even some of the countries that have strongly opposed the invasion of Iraq have agreed to help train the Iraqi security forces and Iraqi Army. As the security situation in Iraq improves over time, and the Iraqi political process moves toward a Constitution and elections, this support should increase.

NATO

A contingent of NATO forces are helping secure the peace in Afghanistan. They have also agreed to assist in the training of the Iraqi armed forces and security forces.

Afghanistan

On balance, the invasion of Afghanistan has been a success. The fundamentalist, radical Taliban government has been overthrown and replaced with a temporary Afghan government – recognized and supported by the UN and NATO – that is rapidly moving toward a final Constitution and an election, probably in early 2005.

Women's rights, which were severely curtailed during the Taliban rule, have been reestablished. Women are now free to go to school and vote in the "new" Afghanistan. More than four million women have already registered to vote.

The large Al Qaeda terrorist training camps have been destroyed and about half of the Al Qaeda leadership killed or captured. Although the Taliban and Al Qaeda organizations are still operating in the tribal regions near the Afghan-Pakistan borders, they are far less capable than they were before the invasion.

Saudi Arabia

The fundamentalist Muslim doctrine adopted by the radical terrorist organizations, "Wahabinism," was born and nourished in Saudi Arabia. In fact, 15 of the 19 hijackers in the 9/11 attacks were Saudis. The major terrorist leader, Osama Bin Laden, is Saudi.

Al Qaeda was originally formed to overthrow the Saudi royal family and turn Saudi Arabia into a fundamentalist Muslim government. However, for many years Al Qaeda turned its attention to targets outside Saudi Arabia, in exchange for the Saudi government "looking the other way," as millions of dollars of support flowed from Saudi businessmen to Al Qaeda.

That deal has now gone sour and Al Qaeda has launched a frenzied attack against the Saudis and foreigners in that country. Saudi Arabia is now cooperating with the U.S. in the War on Terrorism for its own survival. This cooperation has been long overdue. Stability in Saudi Arabia, with its vast oil reserves and strategic location, is in our vital national interests.

Pakistan

Pakistan also has a history of supporting terrorism. The Taliban, which ruled Afghanistan with a strong fundamentalist Muslim government, was supported by Pakistan for many years. Approximately half of the Pakistani population still supports Al Qaeda and the Taliban.

However, Pakistan is now cooperating in the War on Terrorism. Pakistan is a key player in the eventual destruction of Al Qaeda and the capture of Osama Bin Laden. Al Qaeda has designated Pakistan as one of its primary targets. As in other Muslim countries, Al Qaeda leaders want to overthrow the current government and establish a radical, fundamentalist Muslim government.

Libya

Libya, under Colonel Moammar Kaddafi, has long been a country that supported terrorism and was dedicated to developing weapons of mass destruction. The U.S. and the UN imposed strong economic and political sanctions against Libya for its support of international terrorism, and its role in the December 21, 1998 destruction of Pan Am Flight 103 over Lockerbie, Scotland, which killed 259 people aboard the plane and 11 others on the ground. These sanctions significantly hurt the economy of Libya.

After the invasion of Afghanistan and Iraq, Colonel Kaddafi realized he might be next on the list. He has renounced the support of terrorism and the procurement of weapons of mass destruction in exchange for the lifting of sanctions. He stated to the Italian Prime Minister that he "did not want to be the next Iraq." His turnaround was a major win in the War on Terrorism.

Syria

Syria is continuing to support the terrorist movement. The country is a sanctuary for Saddam's henchmen, money, and probably weapons of mass destruction. It fully supports the terrorist groups Hamas and Hezbollah, which have, in effect, full control of Lebanon.

However, Syria is in a tough situation. On one side is the powerful Israeli Army and on the other a U.S. Army Division near its eastern border with Iraq. Syria has a weak economy and is very susceptible to UN and U.S. economic sanctions. Hopefully, these pressures will eventually force Syria to end its support of terrorism. However, Syria has a limited time to reform or it might be the next target for a U.S. air strike or invasion.

Iran

Iran, which is ruled by powerful fundamentalist

Ayatollahs, is our biggest potential enemy in the Mideast. However, there is unrest in Iran by the students, merchants and political reformists. Although the Ayatollahs are in firm control, they are being forced to make some concessions and reforms.

Iran will be in a much weaker position if Iraq is able to form a representative government. Iran also has a growing nuclear weapons program that is a major concern to Israel, the UN, and many European countries. Iran's main concern is that the new Iraqi government be dominated by fellow Shia Muslims and be friendly to Iran, or preferably be controlled by Iran.

Eventually, we must deal with Iran. However, direct military ground action in the near to mid-term is unlikely. Conducting air strikes against Iran's nuclear facilities in the future might be very possible.

Iraq

As discussed in a previous chapter, the decision to invade Iraq was, in my opinion, the correct one, and was a major strike against the international terrorist network. Iraq has been liberated from one of the cruelest dictators in history. Saddam Hussein's Baath Party regime murdered more than 300,000 Iraqis and was responsible for countless other crimes against his people and the people of

> **The decision to invade Iraq was, in my opinion, the correct decision, and was a major strike against the international terrorist network.**

Kuwait and Iran. Saddam has been captured – hiding in a hole like an animal – and will soon go on trial and face justice in full view of an international audience.

The new provisional Iraqi government has been accepted by the vast majority of the Iraqi people and recognized by the UN and by other Muslim countries. The new Iraqi security forces are being formed, trained, and deployed as rapidly as possible. A new Constitution is under construction and free elections will be held sometime in 2005. Despite all the negative reporting, the trends in Iraq are positive.

A Lack of Security

The major remaining problem in Iraq is the very poor security situation. Without good security, the rebuilding of the infrastructure will be greatly hampered, countries will be reluctant to send military forces to Iraq, and the Iraqi people will be reluctant to fully support the new government and participate in the political process.

> **The failure to establish a good security situation [in Iraq] is due to questionable political decisions – not the effectiveness and dedication of the military.**

The American military has done a great job in Iraq under very difficult conditions. The failure to establish a good security situation is due to questionable political decisions – not the effectiveness and dedication of the military. The U.S. attacked with plenty of forces to win the war in the desert.

Saddam's forces were no match for the might of the U.S. military in a conventional desert war.

However, we had an insufficient number and type of forces needed to quickly reestablish law and order and to quell the insurgency after the fall of Baghdad. This lack of forces was well-known to experienced senior military commanders with war-fighting experience (active duty and retired generals) before the invasion. In fact, the Chief of Staff of the Army was fired (retired early) because of his public statements that the invasion force needed to be much larger.

Civilian control of the military is proper and the American tradition. However, in this system, major military decisions are often made by our civilian bosses (sometimes without significant military input) and not our military leaders.

The previous CENT-COM (senior military headquarters responsible for that area of the world) commander, U.S. Marine Corps General Anthony Zinni, stated that his war plan called for more than 300,000 troops to invade Iraq. Our invasion force was comprised of fewer than 100,000. I believe the decision to attack with this small force was a Defense Department decision made by the civilian leadership, and not a military decision.

As a retired U.S. Army General, I can tell you in no uncertain terms that our military is completely controlled by the elected Commander in Chief – the

President – and the appointed officials in the Defense Department. This is the way our Constitution is written and there is no disagreement with this system by the military. Civilian control of the military is proper, and is the American tradition.

However, in this system, major military decisions are often made by our civilian bosses (sometimes without significant military input) and not our military leaders. History is full of examples where the military operation went sour because the civilian officials made decisions that perhaps should have been made by the military.

Some prime examples include: German dictator Adolf Hitler not listening to his generals in World War II; President Lyndon Johnson and Secretary of Defense Robert McNamara making relatively low-level military decisions in the Vietnam War; and Saddam Hussein taking command of his forces in Operation Desert Storm.

"In war there is no substitute for victory."
Douglas MacArthur

The Need for Balance
In every war, there's a delicate balance between who makes what decisions – the military or civilians. In this case, the civilian leadership in the Pentagon relied too much on technology, air power, and poor intelligence.

Another political decision which directly led to the current poor security situation was to disband the Iraqi Army. This left the country with no Iraqi security force and resulted in many of these out-of-work soldiers joining the terrorists.

In addition, the political decision to, in effect, turn the city of Fallujah, a former stronghold of Saddam Hussein, over to the enemy and allow the terrorists to turn it into the center of terrorist activity in Iraq was clearly a civilian and not a military decision. It's difficult to believe that any professional military man would allow the terrorists to have a sanctuary right in the middle of the key combat area.

The hope is that the Iraqi people will now see the terrorist attacks as an anti-Iraqi movement and not a resistance against what many view as an American occupation.

The security decisions are now firmly in the hands of the transitional Iraqi government. The future of Iraq depends on the ability of the new government to get the security situation under control. The hope is that the Iraqi people will now see the terrorist attacks as an anti-Iraqi movement and not a resistance against what many view as an American occupation. The 100,000-plus U.S. forces remaining in Iraq will undoubtedly play a major role in this process but the fight against the terrorists will now have an "Iraqi face."

"In war there is no prize for the runner-up."
General Omar Bradley

The future of Iraq is now clearly in the hands of the Iraqi people —as it should be. They must put aside their regional, tribal, religious, and ethnic differences, and forge a "new Iraq" that is fair and just for all Iraqis. I'm hopeful that, with the help of the United States and other countries in the coalition, they will be successful.

We have made significant progress in winning World War IV, but the outcome is still very much in doubt. It's critical that we continue with our policy of offensive operations against terrorism worldwide. We must not lose our momentum and go on the defensive.

We will not lose this war on the battlefield. We can only lose if the American people succumb to the "Somalia" strategy of the enemy and withdraw their support, due to the length of the war and the high cost in both human and financial terms.

"Victory belongs to the most persevering."
Napoleon Bonaparte

WW IV at a Glance

Based on the majority of media reports we read and hear, it would be easy to conclude that the War on Terrorism being waged by the United States and its allies is, at best, a losing cause, one that's doomed to defeat. However, an objective study of the results to date in many Muslim nations paints quite a different picture. For example, consider the following results that have been achieved to date:

Afghanistan

- On balance, invasion a success.
- Taliban government overthrown and replaced with temporary government moving toward final Constitution and election.
- Women's rights, severely curtailed under Taliban, reestablished.
- Large Al Qaeda terrorist training camps destroyed.
- Many Al Qaeda leaders killed or captured.
- Taliban and Al Qaeda still operating in tribal regions, but far less capably than before.

Saudi Arabia

- Now cooperating in War on Terrorism for its own survival.
- Stability, with vast oil reserves and strategic location, is in vital U.S. interests.

Pakistan

- Now cooperating in War on Terrorism.
- Key player in eventual destruction of Al Qaeda and capture of Bin Laden.

Libya

- Kaddafi has renounced support of terrorism and procurement of WMD.
- Turnaround a major win in War on Terrorism.

Syria

- Caught between Israeli Army on one side and

U.S. Army Division near border with Iraq.
- Weak economy very susceptible to UN and U.S. economic sanctions.
- Hopefully, pressures will force Syria to end terrorist support.
- Has limited time to reform or might be next target for U.S. air strike or invasion.

Iran

- Major unrest by students, merchants and political reformists.
- Ayatollahs being forced to make concessions and reforms.
- Will be in weaker position if Iraq is able to form representative government. Military action in the near- to mid-term unlikely.

Iraq

- Decision to invade Iraq was major strike against international terrorist network.
- Nation liberated from one of cruelest dictators in history.
- Provisional government accepted by vast majority of the people.
- New security forces being formed, trained and deployed as rapidly as possible.
- New Constitution is under construction.
- Free elections sometime in 2005.

CHAPTER 5

FINAL VICTORY: WHAT WILL IT TAKE?

"Freedom from fear and injustice and oppression will be ours only in the measure that men who value such freedom are ready to sustain its possession – to defend it against every thrust from within and without."
Dwight D. Eisenhower

*"A splendid storehouse of integrity and freedom
has been bequeathed to us by our forefathers.
In this day of confusion, of peril to liberty,
our duty is to see that this storehouse
is not robbed of its contents."*
Herbert Hoover

*"It's critical that our people of all political persuasions
realize that we are at war and must combine
our resources and energies in unison
to defeat our enemies."*
Nick Halley

The forces of freedom are on the move for the fourth time in the past 100 years: World War I against the Germans, World War II against Germany and Japan, World War III (the Cold War) against the Soviet Union, and now World War IV against Radical Islam and the countries that support international terrorism.

"If there must be trouble let it be in my day, that my child can have peace."
Thomas Paine

We did *not* choose this war — it was brought to us. We can win this war, but it will be a long and difficult struggle that could last for decades. As citizens, we must do what we always do in a major war — within the freedoms inherent in our Constitution — support our government and the military. The future of our country depends on our actions. Several specific critical ***"DOs and DON'Ts"*** are:

DON'T Judge Progress Based on Casualty Reports

Unfortunately, our military forces have always been required to sacrifice in war. This will always be the case. *However, the hope, prayer and expectation in every war is that the terrible casualties we are suffering now will prevent many more casualties later.* This is the "gamble" we make in every war. The casualties in this war to date have been terrible, but not nearly as high as the rate of casualties we have suffered in our other major shooting wars.

Each casualty in this war is highlighted and receives a great deal of visibility because of our compassion as a nation, but also because this is a political year. Some politicians seeking election have exploited the situation by citing the casualties as evidence that the incumbents have a failed strategy.

If we don't stay on the offensive and defeat this terrible enemy, the next attack, using weapons of mass destruction, could result in the deaths of 300,000 people or more.

In addition, we have a very large, aggressive media who must, day after day, fill 24 hours of air time with the most sensational presentation of the news possible, in order to maximize ratings, and because of the significant media bias against the war.

We need to keep remembering the fact that we lost about 3,000 innocent and unsuspecting people on one day – September 11, 2001. If we don't stay on the offensive and defeat this terrible enemy, the next attack, using weapons of mass destruction, could result in the deaths of 300,000 people or more.

"The tree of liberty must be watered periodically with the blood of tyrants and patriots alike."
Thomas Jefferson

You should not judge the progress of the war by the daily casualty reports. These reports can be very misleading. From a purely military standpoint, high rates are not necessarily bad, and low rates are not necessarily good. During offensive operations, casualties are usually relatively high because the soldiers are attacking the enemy and therefore are in exposed positions. However, attacking the enemy is necessary to win the war.

Because casualties have great political ramifications, military commanders are sometimes "encouraged" to keep casualties low. I have been in these situations as a commander on several occasions, where commanders stay on the defensive and don't expose their soldiers to danger. This keeps the casualty rates down, but allows the enemy to regain the offensive and choose the time and place of their next attacks.

A war cannot be won on the defensive. This often results in increased casualties in the long term. Therefore, by only looking at the casualty rates, it's difficult for the average citizen to determine if we're winning or losing the war.

> **We should grieve with every casualty, but we must realize that these brave men and women in uniform are making the ultimate sacrifice now in order to prevent untold numbers of casualties later in our towns and cities across America.**

The enemy knows we're loving and compassionate people, who place an extremely high value on human life. They're exploiting that sensitivity to try to inflict as many casualties as possible to make us lose faith in the war and withdraw our forces from the battlefields in Afghanistan, Iraq, and many other countries in the world.

Even if we did withdraw, the enemy would see that as a great weakness and come after us even more aggressively on our own soil. We should grieve with every casualty, but we must realize that these brave men and women in uniform are making the ultimate sacrifice now in order to prevent untold numbers of casualties later in our towns and cities across America.

> *"We sleep safely in our beds at night because rough men stand ready to visit violence on those who would do us wrong."*
> George Orwell

DO Put Aside Political Differences and Present a Unified Front Against Radical Islam

We have stood together as a nation in all our successful wars. During the first three, we put our political differences in the background (consistent with our rights as Americans) in order to defeat our foes. In the other conflicts, such as Korea and certainly Vietnam, we did not pull together as a nation and as a result we were not fully successful.

Legitimate political dissent is a critical part of our American way of life. However, this dissent must be done in a responsible way, and not provide encouragement and comfort to our enemies. Our political leaders and their followers must unite and show our enemy that we will not allow terrorists to attack our citizens at home or abroad.

The terrorists might hear us, as free people, debating the strategy and tactics we use, but they must see a united front against their tyranny. Unfortunately, to date in this critical conflict, we're not presenting a united front.

Legitimate political dissent is a critical part of our American way of life. However, this dissent must be done in a responsible way, and not provide encouragement and comfort to our enemies.

In this political year, the terrorists have managed to drive a serious wedge between our political parties. Both parties are slanting and "spinning" the news in order to get elected or reelected. We're conducting numerous and very partisan and acrimonious public hearings about our intelligence failures and who's responsible for the September 11 attacks – *while the war is still in progress* – when we should be discussing how we will defeat our enemies.

This is pure election-year politics, rather than a legitimate search for the truth. This would be like holding hearings, just before the 1944 presidential elections, on the intelligence failures prior to Pearl Harbor, while we were conducting a war on two fronts. It's critical that our people of all political persuasions realize we're at war and must combine our resources and energies in unison to defeat our enemies.

DON'T Have Unrealistic Expectations

This will be a long and difficult war. We must have great patience. The current "baby boomer" generation has made many great contributions to our society. However, one characteristic of this generation is impatience. They want solutions to problems *now*. They want the ninth-inning home run to end the game, the hero to fix the problem *now*, the great battle to end the war *now*.

However, that's *not* the nature of this kind of conflict, in which two completely different political philosophies and social orders are in direct conflict. I sometimes feel we have a "send a man to the moon" curse. Americans and foreigners think: "If Americans can send a man to the moon, then they can accomplish any complicated and complex social or economic endeavor quickly and without significant costs."

For example, Iraq is a country that was ruled by a ruthless dictator for decades. Saddam's policies and the effects of the economic and political sanctions he caused ran the country into the ground. The entire political and material infrastructure in Iraq was in terrible condition. However, many Iraqis and Americans seem to expect that we could rebuild that infrastructure in a few months, when in fact it will take years.

After all, we sent a man to the moon, so we must have almost magical powers. At the end of World War II, we occupied both Germany and Japan and committed a significant number of people and funds to rebuilding their infrastructure and political systems. In both cases, it took more than five years before we were able to return control of their countries to them.

In this case, we turned control back to a provisional Iraqi government *in less than two years*, and have made significant progress in rebuilding the country – particularly when you consider that we're concurrently fighting an insurgency.

We *must* realize that we're in this war for the long term. Iraq, Afghanistan, or any other future campaign in this war, will take time, patience, and determination to successfully accomplish our political and rebuilding objectives.

DO Be Alert

America is an open country with relatively open borders. The security of our borders with Mexico and Canada is very poor. Hundreds of illegal immigrants (or possibly terrorists) cross those borders daily. Only about 10 percent of the thousands of ocean cargo containers that arrive at our ports each day are inspected for illegal contraband.

Our traditions of individual freedoms prevent us from implementing policies that would increase security, but severely restrict individual freedoms and freedom of movement (National ID Cards, profiling of people of Mideast heritage, severely restricting immigration from countries that support or provide terrorists, limiting student visas and work visas from selected countries, etc.).

We're politically correct to the extreme, often to our own detriment. Even the modest provisions in the Patriot Act met with great resistance from many Americans. The new Homeland Security measures will marginally increase our security, but we are very vulnerable to terrorist attacks.

Strange as it may seem to many of us, profiling of any kind is expressly prohibited by government authorities, despite the fact that, over the past 25 years, Muslim male extremists, mostly between the ages of 17 and 40, were responsible for the following atrocities:

- the kidnap and massacre of Olympic athletes during the 1972 Games in Munich;
- the takeover of the U.S. Embassy in Iran in 1979;
- the kidnapping of Americans in Lebanon during the 1980s;
- blowing up the U.S. Marine barracks in Beirut in 1983;
- the hijacking of the cruise ship Achille Lauro in 1985, and the murder of a 70-year-old wheelchair-bound American passenger who was thrown overboard;
- the hijacking of TWA Flight 847 at Athens in 1985;
- the bombing of Pan Am Flight 103 in 1998, killing all passengers and crew members;
- the first bombing of the World Trade Center in 1993;
- the bombing of the U.S. embassies in Kenya and Tanzania in 1998;
- the infamous hijacking of four commercial air-

liners on September 11, 2001, and the resulting murder of thousands of innocent people;
• the kidnap and murder of reporter Daniel
  Pearl in 2002;
• the kidnapping and beheading of innocent
  victims in 2004, compounded by the showing
  of such brutality on worldwide television.

Our last line of defense is our people.
Although profiling is not permitted by law, every
American must be alert to suspicious behavior, such
as: people who seem excessively nervous, upset, or
out of place; people wearing heavy coats in warm
weather; wires protruding from clothes; people who
seem to be taking excessive notice of potential targets
such as critical facilities; cars or vans driving in
unusual ways, or in inappropriate locations, etc. Any
suspicious behavior should be immediately reported
to the local police.

DON'T Overreact to Bad News or Future Terrorist Attacks

In every war, there will be times when things are not
going well for the U.S. The enemy is well trained,
dedicated and determined, and will occasionally have
victories and successes in the war. We must realize
this inevitability and not overreact. Occasional successes by the enemy are unavoidable and don't necessarily signal that our policies and strategies are
faulty, or that any of our officials or military leaders
are incompetent.

On other occasions, there will be setbacks

caused by our own military personnel. Two examples of this are friendly fire incidents and scandals such as the Abu Ghraib prison camp disaster in Iraq, where several of our military police and interrogators abused Iraqi prisoners.

Friendly fire incidents, where Americans become casualties at the hands of our own soldiers, are not acceptable, but these incidents happen in every war. When you combine lethal weapons, fatigued soldiers and the "fog of war," these incidents will happen.

The prison camp scandal was terrible and totally unacceptable, involving a few rogue soldiers who committed acts that are completely inconsistent with our American values and morals. The participants should be thoroughly investigated and the guilty punished.

The most upset people I observed during this incident were the members of our armed forces. They work around the clock at great risk, striving to do the right things for our country. Incidents such as the prison camp scandal dominate the news and bring discredit to our great military people – 99.999 percent of whom are doing their duty properly and making us proud.

The terrorists believe Americans are weak. We have never had to endure repeated terrorist attacks in our own country. The terrorist group Al Qaeda has a doctrine that Americans will always make the final damage from any terrorist attack one hundred times worse than the actual damage.

The 9/11 attacks were devastating but we

made them much worse by our reactions. We had many people cancel vacations, not go to public events, postpone major purchases, and alter their lifestyles in many other ways. In addition, there was a panic selling of stocks which caused a great drop in the stock market, costing investors billions of dollars.

We must realize the enemy counts on us to overreact to all the bad news. We must steel ourselves for these reverses and terrorist attacks, and not make any situation worse by our overreaction to events. The strength of a nation is measured by its reaction to hard times. Our nation has endured great hardship and adversity for more than 200 years. We must remember our heritage and our strength as a nation, and remain strong during times of adversity.

CHAPTER 6

SUCCESS OR FAILURE: THE CHOICE IS OURS!

"Peace, like war, can succeed only where
there is a will to enforce it,
and where there is available power to enforce it."
Franklin Delano Roosevelt

"In peace nothing so becomes a man
as modest stillness and humility;
but when the blast of war blows in our ears,
then imitate the actions of the tiger."
William Shakespeare

"We can win this war!
We must win this war, and provide
security and freedom from terrorism
to the world throughout the 21st century."
Nick Halley

The fundamental danger to our country in the 21st century is the threat that radical Islam fanatics and the rogue countries that support them will obtain and use weapons of mass destruction (chemical, biological and nuclear) against our country and the other countries in the free world. This is the number one national security issue we face in the foreseeable future.

To counter this threat, we have developed a new strategy – preemption. This is a very dangerous strategy that requires excellent intelligence, and calls for aggressive combat operations when there's a clear and present danger to our country. This is the only viable strategy against a foe that cannot be deterred by our military might. In order to protect our citizens from terrorist attacks, we must continue to apply this aggressive strategy worldwide.

Americans must understand that we are the only superpower in the world, and the only force that can counter the radical international terrorist movement.

"If we desire to avoid insult, we must be able to repel it; if we desire to secure peace, one of the most powerful instruments of our rising prosperity, it must be known that we are at all times ready for war."
George Washington

Americans must understand that we are the

only superpower in the world, and the only force that can counter the radical international terrorist movement. We no longer have the geographical protection of the great expanses of the Atlantic and Pacific oceans. We cannot afford to withdraw into a "fortress America" mentality, protect our own country, and believe we can continue to enjoy our "American way of life."

We are a vulnerable nation, with relatively open borders. The terrorists are at war with us and will continue to attack America, until and unless they are defeated once and for all.

> *"To sit back hoping that some day, some way, someone will make things right is to go on feeding the crocodile, hoping that he will eat you last – but eat you he will."*
> *Ronald Reagan*

The nations that are appeasing the terrorists by not participating in the current central battlegrounds in Iraq and Afghanistan will eventually suffer massive attacks.

A Global Effort

We must continue to "globalize" the war, by enlisting the aid of every country threatened by terrorism. Some of our European allies – particularly France, Germany, Russia, and Spain – will soon realize the terrorists are at war with every "infidel" or non-believer nation.

Spain reacted to a

series of terrorist attacks by replacing the anti-terrorist government with an appeasement government. The terrorists have almost defeated the Spanish. The French are probably next. They're particularly vulnerable because of their large (15 percent) and growing Muslim population.

The nations that are appeasing the terrorists by not participating in the current central battlegrounds in Iraq and Afghanistan will eventually suffer massive attacks and only then fully commit their military forces to this cause. Hopefully, it will not be too late before they act.

The current appeasement policy of some European countries – particularly France – is similar to the appeasement of Adolf Hitler's expansionist strategy prior to World War II. Many European countries hoped that, by appeasing Hitler and not opposing his annexation of neighboring countries, he would eventually be satisfied. However, radical movements are never satisfied until they obtain total victory.

> **Radical movements are never satisfied until they obtain total victory.**

> *"It is fatal to enter any war without the will to win."*
> **General Douglas MacArthur**

Defeat Not an Option
If we were to lose this war, or if we lose our will and withdraw our forces worldwide, the results would be

devastating. One by one, the Muslim countries would be converted to fundamentalist governments that would be extremely hostile to the United States; we would no longer be the premier country in the world.

The attacks on our soil would greatly increase. Israel would cease to exist. Al Qaeda would control the majority of the world's oil supply and hence have a profound impact on the world economy. Hundreds of thousands of radical young men and women would be available to fight any place in the world, as determined by the radical Islamic religious leaders.

We must not and cannot consider losing as an option. In the early 1900s, the British fought the Boers in South Africa – The Second Boer War. Early in the war, things were not going well for the British. The Queen of England, Queen Victoria, was getting a rather dismal briefing from her generals on the losses being suffered by the British.

She stopped the briefing in mid-sentence, stood up from her throne and in a very dramatic voice said: *"We are not interested in the possibilities of defeat; those possibilities do not exist."*

We must develop the same attitude. Defeat is not an option we should ever consider.

The Greatest Generation

The World War II generation has been correctly labeled "the greatest generation," standing up to the forces of fascism and tyranny, and winning the peace through great determination and sacrifice. Our current generation is facing an equally dangerous foe that's threatening our way of life. We must now "stand up and be counted," and become an even "greater generation."

We can only lose this war by allowing the enemy to divide us as a people and break our will by continuing to inflict casualties on U.S. citizens and soldiers over time.

We *can* win this war! We *must* win this war, and provide security and freedom from terrorism to the world throughout the 21st century. The key to winning is having the strength, the will and the determination to fight the forces of radical Islam until we are victorious.

CHAPTER 7

LEADERSHIP: THE KEY TO VICTORY!

*"Victory, Victory at all costs, victory in spite of terror,
victory, however long and hard the road may be,
for without victory there is no freedom."*
Winston Churchill

"Leadership is a great burden. We grow weary of it at times…But if we are not to shoulder the burdens of leadership in the free world, then who will? The alternatives are neither pleasant nor acceptable."
Ronald Reagan

"During these difficult times of international terrorism, it's critical for our leaders to show strength, so we can as a nation present a strong front and collectively stand up to terrorism and show – that because of our great leadership which gives us strength and resolve – the terrorists cannot defeat America and the free world."
Nick Halley

During the darkest days early in World War II, the German Army had overrun Western Europe and was threatening to invade England across the very narrow fifteen-mile-wide English Channel. London was being mercilessly bombed every night by hundreds of German bombers. The situation was very grim.

The British people needed a boost in their morale during these very dark days. The British Prime Minister, Winston Churchill, was a great inspirational leader, orator and motivational speaker. At this critical moment in history, he assembled his key political and military leaders in an underground bunker complex near London and gave a very short but very powerful speech.

The last lines of that speech, "Victory at all costs, victory in spite of terror, victory, however long and hard the road may be" are completely applicable to the situation the free world faces against international terrorism today. We are fighting for our survival as a free nation and it's necessary for us to stay strong and win this war, "in spite of terror, and however long and hard the road may be."

Prime Minister Churchill clearly provided great leadership and inspiration to his people at a very critical time in their history. Our leaders – at all levels – must now provide similar leadership and inspiration for our people.

Leadership is the Key
When you've got a battle to fight, leadership deter-

mines the winner. In every war in history, leadership has been a critical factor in determining the winner. In the war against terrorism, leadership will be the key to victory. This crucial leadership must be provided not only by our political and military leaders but also by leaders from all parts of our society – business leaders at all levels, religious leaders, media executives, academic leaders and family leaders.

Leadership is challenging under even the most favorable conditions. During times of war or under stress, being a good leader is much more difficult. However, the basic leadership principles during both war and peace (good times or difficult times) are basically the same. Only the difficulty in practicing these principles changes. In my book, *Leadership Under Fire*, I present a detailed study on the subject of leadership.

"Be willing to make decisions.
That's the most important quality of a good leader.
Don't fall victim to what I call the ready-aim-aim-
aim syndrome. You must be willing to fire."
T. Boone Pickens

Leading by Example Under Fire

One of the most important leadership principles – leading by example – becomes even more critical during times of strife. People always look to their leaders for guidance and inspiration but, during times of strife, they depend on them to an even greater degree. Leading by example means leaders take charge and set the standards for their followers by their actions and attitudes. A leader who truly leads by example creates an atmosphere that inspires people and gives them confidence.

The "leads by example" leader operates well above the minimum standards and sets the example in all areas by courage, coolness under fire, conduct, sense of responsibility, integrity, fairness and attitude.

"When put in charge, take charge."
Major General Max Thurman

Leadership from business leaders will be particularly critical in this war. We live in a capitalistic society. Our businesses are the backbone – the front lines – of the American economic system. In many ways, our businesses are also the front lines against terrorism. The terrorists are well aware of our vulnerabilities in this area and are specifically targeting their terrorist attacks to cripple or damage our economy.

"There was never a world in greater need of men and women who know the way, and can keep ahead and draw others to follow."
Samuel M. Zwemer

Business leaders have a great responsibility to protect their businesses by carefully screening their employees and ensuring that only authorized people have access to their establishments. In addition, after the inevitable next terrorist attacks, they must provide great leadership – both inside and outside their organizations — to ensure that the terrorists' goal of damaging our economies by our overreaction to those attacks is not successful. As mentioned previously, the terrorists depend on us overreacting to their attacks and making the actual inflicted damage much more severe.

Our family leaders also have a very critical leadership role. Terror attacks are designed to intimidate and frighten our civilian population. The terrorists specifically target family members — including children. The family leaders — fathers, mothers and older children — must provide great leadership within their families to minimize the fear, tension and strife caused by these terrible attacks.

During these difficult times of international terrorism, it's critical for all our national, business and family leaders to show strength, and to lead by example under pressure. We must have strong families, strong businesses and a strong national resolve, so that we can as a nation collectively stand up to terrorism and show that — because of our great leadership — the terrorists cannot defeat America and the free world.

ABOUT THE AUTHOR

Brigadier General Nick Halley (U.S. Army, Retired) is a recognized expert on leadership and terrorism. He has commanded thousands of our soldiers in combat in three conflicts – Vietnam, Grenada, and Desert Storm. He is an army paratrooper, army ranger and special operations veteran. He has been awarded many significant decorations, including two Silver Stars for bravery in combat actions, four Bronze Stars, and two Purple Hearts for wounds in combat operations.

In addition to his combat commands, General Halley has had a wide variety of assignments, including assistant professor of mathematics at West Point, assignments to the U.S. embassies in both Korea and Japan, and many years with the Army's premier fighting division – the 82nd Airborne Division.

His final active duty assignment was the Commanding General of the XVIIIth Airborne Corps artillery and rocket forces in Desert Storm, where he commanded tens of thousand of our soldiers in the most challenging leadership environment – combat. Since his retirement from the Army, General Halley has had a distinguished civilian career at the director/vice president/general manager level with several prestigious international electronics firms, including Motorola.

General Halley is a graduate of the United States Military Academy at West Point, and holds a master's degree in nuclear physics from the University of Virginia. Currently, he is the on-air military and terrorism expert for WGN-TV in Chicago, which is seen nationwide on cable.

TO ORDER BOOKS

Books can be ordered directly for $14.00 from the author at:

Website: www.generalnickspeaks.com
Telephone: 847-719-2637
Email: nickhalley@msn.com

The book can also be purchased through Amazon at www.amazon.com

Bulk discount rates are also available by contacting General Halley by telephone, email or through his website.